MAKE A TOUCHDOWN OF YOUR LIFE
24 Keys to Crossing the Goal Line of Success

MAKE A TOUCHDOWN OF YOUR LIFE

Published in the United States by:

Kory Minor
Kory Minor Industries (KMI)
1004 West Covina Parkway, #246
West Covina, CA 91790

DISCLAIMER
The information contained in this book is based upon the research and personal and professional experiences of the author. While the publisher and author have used their best efforts in preparing this book, they make no representations or warranties with respect to the accuracy or completeness of the contents of this book and specifically disclaim any implied warranties of merchantability or fitness for a particular purpose. It is not intended as a substitute for consulting with a professional. You should consult with a professional where appropriate.

ACKNOWLEDGEMENTS

First and foremost, I give all glory and honor to God for giving me life, a knack of being transparent, and the ability to touch millions of lives on my quest.

My reason for being is *because of eight amazing and inspiring people* who have tremendously blessed me in countless ways. I would like to thank my courageous and wonderful mother, Kim, who I could never repay for her dedicated watch over me. To the best grandparents in the world, Betty and Wardell, I thank you from the bottom of my heart. The two of you raised me like your own.

To my beautiful wife, Lisa, thank you for being with me through thick and thin. You are my true supporter, confidant, best friend, and eternal true love. Also, I would like to thank my sister, Koi, whose musical talents are endless. Last but not least, I would like to thank my three amazing children, Ilyanna, Noah, and Julian. The three of you are the reason I breathe every day.

With Love,

Kory Minor

CONTENTS

MAKE A TOUCHDOWN OF YOUR LIFE

FOREWORD

Many years ago I traveled to Southern California to recruit one of the most talented senior football players in the country.

Little did I realize the positive impact Kory Minor would have on the students at Notre Dame as well as our football team. Even today, I remember vividly what a loving home Kory came from. He had a loving mother who obviously had instilled the values that made Kory a success both on and off the field.

One of the qualities I looked for in a potential football player was the respect he showed for his elders, the law, people in positions of authority and his mother. Kory excelled in all these areas.

So many times when a great high school prospect gets to college, he loses his desire to be great. This was the opposite of Kory. He arrived with a desire to excel both on the field and in the classroom, and he accomplished both. Kory started for us as a freshman at Notre Dame and did very well as a student. Kory went on to start for four years at Notre Dame and played several years in the NFL.

However, it wasn't his exceptional athletic talent that made Kory Minor one of the most memorable players I coached, but it was the intangible qualities that made him special. He has one of the most engaging personalities you will ever meet. He loves people and they immediately love him. He cared about people and he showed it. He was also very goal oriented in every phase of his life.

He arrived at Notre Dame with a maturity level beyond his years. I desire for our players to live by three rules. 1) Do right, 2) Do your best at all times, and 3) Show people you care.

When you follow these 3 rules, you will always be the type of person that others can trust, know you are committed to excellence and that you care about them. Kory always exhibited these 3 qualities.

However, the one quality that Kory exhibited at all times was that he was a happy person. I have never seen him down, depressed or feeling sorry for himself.

I know of very few people in this world more qualified to write this self-help book than Kory Minor. I look forward to buying his book as I want to find out what the secret is to Kory's success and happiness.

I will make 5 assumptions about you.

1. You want to go to heaven.

2. You want to be happy and successful in your personal life.

3. You want to be successful professionally.

4. You want to feel needed and loved.

5. You want to feel secure about your future.

If these assumptions are true about you, then you must read Kory Minor's book, Make A Touchdown Of Your Life. You will be glad you did and your life will change for the better.

Lou Holtz

REASONS WHY YOU SHOULD READ THIS BOOK

If you desire something greater or are tired of being unhappy and unfulfilled, you need to read this book.

The information here will alert you to some of the most common mistakes people, like you, make in their pursuit of success.

You are probably unknowingly making a few of these "success blunders" right now. **Any one of these mistakes will cost you opportunities, joy, and financial freedom.**

But, *by discovering these often-overlooked mistakes and strategies*, you will avoid these dangers and **essentially guarantee yourself more happiness, success, and fulfillment - now and in your future.**

It's a fact that degrees and diplomas won't bring you the freedom, money, or success that's rightfully yours.

Only the right knowledge and actions will. *These are the only two things standing between you and your desires.*

Now, you can **find out easily and quickly what successful athletes, CEO's, and billionaires know.**

[4]

You'll also be exposed to what they do in order to achieve GREATNESS. The strategies and actions you'll uncover in this book will give you *the knowledge and the "how-to" necessary to live your dreams.*

This book might not be for you, **UNLESS** you are:

- **Eager for a change...**

- **Tired of not being happy...**

- **Hungry for something greater...**

- **Ready to take proven actions...**

If you're ready to unleash your inner GREATNESS and are **tired of being told that you can't,** this book is for you!

You'll discover things like:

- **The Power of Sleepless Nights:** Learn why *the very things that keep you up at night might be your ticket to success.*

- **The True Calling of Your Soul:** Amazing results come to you when you're in alignment with this success principle. *Do you know why?*

- **Love Thy Haters:** No, this isn't one of the Ten Commandments, but just about every successful person uses it. *Learn why successful people smile* *at their haters and how you can handle the naysayers who try to kill your dreams.*

- **Your Driving Force:** *Find out how to create and harness* the power that will make your success journey worth it for you, *especially when things get hard.*

- **The "All In" Mindset:** How to adopt the mindset of professional athletes that gets them in the game and off the sidelines.

- **Newton's Third Law of Motion:** One of the most important keys to your success lies here. Only *when you apply it to your life will you get real results.*

- **Unleashing Your Greatness:** Discover *why you can't afford **not** to* unleash your full potential and also how doing so will *rid you of a great deal of emotional pain.*

- **Your Golden Vision:** Every Olympic and professional athlete uses a "golden vision." *Do you?*

- **And MUCH More**

WHY I WROTE THIS BOOK

You know how most people are – they're busy and are working hard 12 months of the year, yet they are practically no closer to success.

I am determined to change that.

Most people allow fear to stop them dead in their tracks. They settle for average or second best instead of grabbing hold of their dreams and GREATNESS. *Does this sound a little like you?*

I was blessed, since I was a preschooler, with a relentless determination to be great. **Like you, my life has had its challenges and obstacles.** Nevertheless, I overcame them and have continually attained my goals – goal after goal, and dream after dream.

This book is one of many ways for me to give back to the millions of people who still hunger for success. *Are you one of those people? **Are you still hungry?***

Life can be tough and many people reach a point where they are *constantly plagued by a feeling of low energy and frustration.* **The clear-cut and easy to understand strategies found in this book will empower and energize you** to take the RIGHT actions necessary for YOUR success. My goal is to help you:

- Understand you are the key to your success

- Become more than average

- Earn more money, and increase your income and wealth

- Reach your dream or dreams

- Take action into your own hands

- Find fulfillment and happiness

- Get what you want

- Find your WHY

Instead of letting life and opportunities pass you by, **I challenge you to live life on your own terms.** There's no need to put off your success or greatness another day.

- Are you just drifting in the wind?

- Do you want to make a difference?

- Do past mistakes or present shortcomings have you stuck?

- Have you given up on discovering your purpose or calling in life?

- Do the haters and naysayers distract you?

- Have you ever wanted to know what happy, successful, and rich folks do that you don't?

- Are you sick and tired of settling for less?

[8]

- Would you like to experience more of what life has waiting for you?

Make a Touchdown of Your Life

If your answer is "yes" to any of these questions, then you are the reason I wrote this book.

You are one of many people who will benefit from the *no-nonsense and easy-to-implement knowledge within these pages.* Before you **begin discovering the life-changing principles here**, <u>look in the mirror</u>. What you see is more than enough to achieve GREATNESS.

Don't be afraid to be great. Don't be afraid to shoot for the stars. Don't be afraid to shoot for the moon. If you can live without being afraid to be great, <u>you will find life so much more rewarding.</u>

You are the reason I wrote this book.

In it are the **insights, action steps, and inspiration necessary for you to be great.** It's time for you to go forth, live your dreams, and find your success!

WHY AM I QUALIFIED TO WRITE THIS BOOK

Like you, I'm very familiar with *the fear of failure* – it's my worst fear and a strong motivator.

Regardless of fear, I have achieved everything I've put my mind to thus far, including playing in the National Football League (NFL) and being a successful business owner.

I grew up in a single parent household. During my preschool years, I picked out my college. Watching the Fighting Irish football games every week made Notre Dame my destiny, even though the chances of my mother being able to cover my tuition were slim to none. I was dedicated and worked hard on the gridiron honing my talents in high school and was named the USA Today Defensive Player of the Year - college tuition was no longer an issue. Despite having plenty of options, there was no doubt I was heading to Notre Dame where I started for Coach Lou Holtz as a freshman and was a star defensive player and team captain.

After only 3½ years, I graduated with a Business degree in marketing and was drafted by the San Francisco 49ers. Subsequently, I played four years for the Carolina Panthers. This wasn't where my dream ended though because I wanted to be a business owner. Imagine yourself playing for an NFL team, having a glamorous lifestyle and a promising future. If you look around an NFL locker room, you will find plenty of men who are taking full advantage of what that life has to offer. Would it be easy to turn your back on that?

My wonderful NFL career was just a means of survival until I was ready to live my real dream of being a business owner. During the off-season, I didn't kick back and relax, but was busy with business internships. I gave up a guaranteed comfortable lifestyle to follow my dream after realizing that football had become just a job. *The decision wasn't hard – do something that I loved – so I took the leap.*

After dabbling in the stock market and exploring other opportunities, I finally decided to buy a franchise despite having never run a business before. To make my initial business venture even more challenging, I found myself operating a consumer-driven franchise in the middle of an economic meltdown. I kept a positive attitude, won several sales competitions, and was selected to be in some of the franchise's national commercials. Within two years, I expanded my ownership to five restaurants. I've been able to achieve my goals without stepping on anyone or sacrificing my sense of self. No matter what,

I've held my integrity intact and never given up on my dreams.

I share my story here with you not to boast, but rather to show you my qualifications for writing this book. In addition to my experience with professional football and business, I am a:

- Motivational coach, author, and speaker

- Seminar and corporate workshop leader

- Creator of comprehensive audio and online courses

A family man and a big dreamer with a "glass half-full" mentality is a fair description of me. On my journey to success, I have remained focused on my vision and overcome many challenges. *My goal for this book is to share my unique and proven insights, strategies, and techniques with you so that you too can reach your dreams.*

To contact Kory Minor, or to be placed on a mailing list for updates about new programs and information that will help you become great and experience more success, visit his website: www.KoryMinor.com.

[12]

Pre-Game

"Believing that you are 'great' starts with the conversation you have in your mind."

OPEN YOUR HEART & MIND TO UNLIMITED POTENTIAL

You have the potential for GREATNESS. And even though some downer-types might be quick to point out that not everyone can be the guy who makes the game-winning touchdown, that doesn't mean you have to listen to them. This is especially true if those downer-types are in your own head.

What keeps you up at night?

Do you spend sleepless nights tossing and turning, wishing that you were living someone else's life?

Have the childhood dreams that you can be anything you want to be and do anything you want to do completely evaporated, leaving you feeling tackled by life, like you need to be dragged from the gridiron on a stretcher?

It's time to turn off the voices that say, "I can't" and bring those dreams to fruition. After all, your unlimited potential has been patiently waiting to see you win in your game of life. It's time for you to get in the game and win.

Are you ready to unleash your full potential?

The first step toward success is realizing that setbacks are nothing more than life lessons.

International speaker and author Willie Jolley said, "A setback is a setup for a comeback." That's the attitude you must adopt if you want to unleash your full potential. It's easy to assume that those who've made it big didn't encounter any setbacks; however, every successful person has had to comeback from countless setbacks in order to achieve their GREATNESS.

If you let the things that seem like roadblocks prevent you from reaching your full potential, you are not only punishing yourself, but the people around you as well.

Your family depends on you to be the best you can be, whether it's your parents, who did their best to instill in you a sense of self-worth and aspiration, or your spouse and children, who look to you as the provider. When you let them down, you fail yourself. And you're worth more than that.

Forget regret

Everyone's made mistakes. But in order to move forward, you have to release the feelings of regret that come from those mistakes. A mistake doesn't mean failure. In fact, decide now that failure is not an option.

For successful people, nothing that may resemble failure is an end. Instead it's just a chance to make another attempt, one that is much more likely to succeed.

Have you made a difference thus far?

When Magic Johnson learned he was HIV-positive, he could have allowed it to send him into a deep depression. He could have holed up until the entire country had forgotten his place as one of the most legendary basketball players to hit the court. Instead, he used his fame as a pedestal and became one of the most well-known voices of AIDS. And in doing so, he attracted enough attention and raised enough money through his charitable foundation that HIV is no longer the death sentence that it once was.

His setback became something bigger than himself. He became a living tribute to the idea that everything happens for a reason. That is the most powerful way to see those things that might initially appear as setbacks.

You just need to tackle them head-on before they get the chance to tackle you. Whatever your situation and resources, you can make a difference.

Are you just drifting in the wind?

When people ask you what you do, you want to be proud of the answer rather than fumbling around, stuttering something inaudible, and slinking away in embarrassment.

You were given life as a great gift, and the universe doesn't want you to waste it. Let's be honest here. You don't want to waste it either. You are here on this earth as part of a single unit, a whole that suffers when one part is out of alignment.

So, it's time to accept your role and the challenges that life offers, rather than drifting along like a piece of dust or a tumbleweed on a lazy summer breeze, aimless and bound for nowhere.

Recognize that you, as much as anyone else, deserve to be happy and successful.

Instant karma

Begin by infusing your world with good karma, paying it forward to create an environment that encourages good things.

- Hold a door for the person behind you.

- Pay the toll for the next car in your lane.

- Bring cupcakes to share with your coworkers. (You can buy them if the oven is not your friend.)

- Offer a smile and be kind instead of barking at the clerk manning the busy store checkout.

- Start a conversation with the person next to you on the bus. You might learn something new in the process.

- Stop by a lonely neighbor's apartment with a portion of your family dinner. Many older people don't cook for themselves and would really appreciate a hot meal.

After a while, your feelings of self-worth will rise and you'll get to know yourself better. You'll begin opening your heart and mind to discovering the path your life was ultimately meant to take.

Call to action

Open your heart and mind to unlimited potential. Realize that what's keeping you up at night might just be your ticket to success. Regardless of past mistakes or any present shortcomings, you still have vast amounts of untapped potential.

Reflect on your life and current position. Where can you make a difference? You have tons more to give.

What does this mean for your life?

_____

_____

_____

_____

_____

1st Quarter

"The best way to ignite confidence is by doing what you fear the most."

1st Down: Vision

"The key ingredient in setting goals is visualizing yourself achieving them."

Let's suppose you are going to take a cross-country drive from California to Florida. What are the main items you need for the trip? You would probably want to take food, clothes, and a few other personal items. But, what about a map? How important do you think a map would be? From my point of view, the map is a necessity and probably the most important item. Why?

The map represents the Vision for your trip. It's the tool that helps you stay focused on and moving towards your destination. The map lets you know exactly where to turn. It provides an indication of the distance between mile markers. Your map also serves as the key instrument necessary for you to reach your destination on time. The map is truly *a necessary tool.* Wouldn't you agree?!

Your vision serves as *a masterpiece of your life before* your dream comes into existence. Vision allows you to see all of the things you want in life while at the same time deterring you from the things you don't want. Life has beaten many strong men, especially those without a vision. Creating your vision will allow you to remain strong and keep fighting when life gets tough.

[23]

Successful athletes have always embraced and used visions. Imagine a 100M female sprinter. By the time she is down in the blocks ready to go, she has already envisioned, time and time again, every breath and every step she will take in her race toward the white tape.

The great thing about your Vision is that you can create it whenever and however you see fit. Don't worry that you might start out with one goal in mind, and a year later, decide to alter it. Just the fact that you've started on the journey to realizing your vision will cause your momentum to skyrocket.

After you've created your vision, never lose sight of it. If you do, it may prove difficult, if not impossible, for you to survive, stay focused, and thrive.

Think about your life. Do you plan on getting from "A" to "Z" without a Vision or clear plan? If so, how do you plan to do it? Helen Keller said, "It's a terrible thing to see and have no Vision." If you are going to achieve what you strongly desire and what is rightfully yours on this earth, your Vision has to be Big, Strong, and Bold! Only then will it be able to push and pull you forward when you feel like quitting!

Today, think about your Vision, establish your plan, and take over the world like I know you can!

Good Luck and Commit to Being Great!!!

[24]

THE TRUE CALLING OF YOUR SOUL

"If it takes the words of someone else to motivate you then you have to ask yourself is this really what I want?"

Without knowing what direction you're meant to go, it's hard to start the journey. Revealing your true calling – what the universe means for you to do – is one of the essentials to getting into formation for a successful, enriching life.

And although it might sound a bit esoteric or mysterious, the key to finding your success is to tap into your deepest dreams and desires.

Our reason for being

Everyone imagines that they are here for a reason. When survivors defy the odds and overcome deadly circumstances, they almost always say they felt like they survived because they had not yet fulfilled their life's destiny and purpose. It was not their time to go.

At its core, everyone is here to live their life with joy, making every day count in some way. The universe does not expect anyone to drag themselves to a dull, boring job and then back home again; even more depressed and downtrodden than when they initially left. There's more to it all than that.

So how do you define your purpose?

When you close your eyes, what do you envision for yourself? What are the dreams and desires that hold your attention? What have you always imagined you'd become? I bet it's not a gig as a checker at the local dollar store.

When Oprah Winfrey was still in high school, a time when most teens are still wondering about their futures, she landed a job at a local radio station. She knew from a very early age that she wanted more out of life. She didn't let her tragic childhood setbacks – including a rape at age 9 and a pregnancy that ended in a stillbirth at age 14 – envelop her in misery.

Instead, she recognized the gifts she had been given and before she was even out of her teens moved up to co-anchor her local TV station's evening news.

Now, one of the most celebrated women in the entertainment industry, Winfrey has used her fame to transform the lives of women worldwide. She has helped them accept themselves by sharing publicly her own personal struggles with weight, racial tensions, and romance.

Winfrey probably saw her life's purpose as being "to change the world." In some way, on some level, that's why everyone is here on this earth.

Everyone is meant to make a difference, to live up to God's plan and improve the universe, one action and one person at a time.

Finding your calling can produce amazing results

When you're doing the things you love to do, time ceases to exist. It doesn't drag or seem to stop entirely; it just doesn't seem to be. When you are doing what you love, your heart sings.

And it is in those moments when you can find GREATNESS.

When you're in the zone, having broken through the wall and hit your stride, anything seems possible. That is where success lies. That is where you can produce amazing results.

If you have any doubts about your true calling, go back in time to a more innocent point in your life; a time when life's responsibilities and problems had yet to make a big impact on how you saw your role in the world. Doing that will help you see the direction you are meant to go.

Are you aligned with the universe?

The thing is, just as doing what you are meant to do can bring success, doing something that is not in keeping with your gifts and talents can drag you down.

Be truly honest with yourself. If you're not happy, you know that you're not meant to do whatever it is you're doing.

If you hate going to work every day and you have to force yourself out the door and into the car each morning, something isn't right. Take a cue from Peter Gibbons, the main character in "Office Space." When he realized he was miserable, he went after his new life with vigor, taking what was ultimately meant to be his.

When you're doing the right job, it will feel like no job at all. Everything will come more easily and with more joy. When you're aligned with the universe, your work becomes play.

Call to action

GREATNESS is yours for the taking. To make today and the next day better, accept that your dream or goals are meant for you. Then, do all you can to make them happen.

Follow the true calling of your soul. Do what you love to do. Live your life with purpose and enjoy every minute of it. Doing these things will open the door to a new realm called "anything is possible."

What does this mean for your life?

_____

_____

_____

_____

_____

WHERE DOES YOUR PASSION LIE?

"True passion lies in your heart and soul."

With joy in place, you can become more in tune with both your true desires and that essential key – finding your passion. This allows you to better map out your path in life.

It's the things you love the most that create the stepping-stones for making this happen. People who don't take advantage of the gifts they were born with are usually the ones who have the most difficultly finding their way in life.

What do you love best?

To truly target that joy, make smart use of your God-given talents. Recall the things you gravitated toward as a child.

A great way to do this is to make a list. Write down everything you're good at and all the things you loved to do when you were a kid. If your list includes model airplanes, maybe an aeronautics degree is in your future. If you loved to swim, teaching classes at the YMCA could be your true calling.

Looking at a new love

In addition to considering those childhood pleasures, it's important to also look at what you love to do today.

Do you spend all your free time in the garden, growing prize-winning vegetables that you put up for winter? Why not create an innovative tomato salsa recipe that you might be able to sell to some of your favorite neighborhood restaurants? Don't let having a small kitchen stop you. Contact your local Chamber of Commerce and see if they can help you find regulation-quality space to rent at a community center or school.

Maybe you find yourself at the park most weekends playing football with friends and reliving your glory days on the high school field. Grab that ball and run with it, because the dream doesn't have to be over, even if almost everyone says that it should be. Your blogs about football could attract the attention of a national news outlet or a local peewee league in need of a new coach.

Add to the list things you want to do, whether that means giving an endowment to your favorite charity or landing a job at your favorite radio station. Really, here's the chance to be creative. If you love hot dogs, consider adding "Dethrone Nathan's Hot Dog Eating Champ" to the list. With a record of eating 62 dogs (and buns) in10 minutes under his belt, Joey Chestnut could use the competition. Somewhere among all the things on your list, you'll find a guide to what you were meant to do.

Are you hungry enough?

Being equipped with powerful success guidelines and sage advice is not enough. You must have a strong desire. You must really want it. You must be hungry.

Motivational speaker and respected author Les Brown is well known for his phrase "you gotta be hungry!" His deep hunger took him from broke and essentially homeless to earning millions of dollars each year. Les Brown knows from experience that without his hunger, he would have given up on his dream of becoming one of the highest paid motivational speakers of the 1990's.

Why must you be hungry? Because it's going to take a lot of work, with time spent every day doing your best, to make it happen. Many people make the mistake of assuming that achieving their goals will be easy or they underestimate how much effort and work is required to realize their dreams. That's the type of mindset responsible for so many people giving up. When these "easy" minded folks come up against hard work, they often quit because they aren't mentally or otherwise prepared to push through those difficult moments.

Don't make that mistake. Know and expect that it's going to be downright hard at times. Be prepared to put in the work. After all, if it were easy, then everybody would be doing it, right? If it were easy, then everyone would be living their dreams and you would have already arrived at your goals. Accepting the "hard work" aspect of success is necessary if you actually want to attain your aspirations and goals.

You'll make sacrifices that require more than a few moments or a few hours. You'll have to give up some precious things in order to reach your dream.

The successful people you most admire invest months and years working toward a single goal, not letting the voices in their heads (as well as voices outside their heads) detract them from their mission.

Chicago Bears legend Walter Peyton developed his strength on the football field by moving dirt. This summer training camp of sorts was crafted by his mother. She created the project as a way to keep her sons out of trouble and likely never imagined it would lead to a football career. But Peyton used his childhood discipline as a way to excel not only at the game, but also at academics, creating a complete package that was appealing to National Football League execs.

He knew what it would take to be a success. He dug deep, making time for sports as well as hitting the books, proving his hunger at every turn.

All in a day's work

Athletes spend hours a day working out, chiseling their bodies into well-oiled machines.

At no time do they question the end goal or their path to get there. They know that hard work is essential. Without putting in the time, they can never get where they're going.

Successful people, like extraordinary athletes, know that you can't fake it. They know a secret that's available to everyone: You must devote not only your mind, body, and spirit to your goal, but also your time.

A great way to determine whether you're committed to a chosen vision or dream is to take a tally of your time and finances.

- Track your finances. You can do so for a week, a month, or a year. See where your money goes. If you're not devoting any hard-earned cash to your vision, then it's not a real vision. It's just a wish.

- Track your time. A couple days worth will do, although tracking it for one week will really shock you. You'll be surprised at both where your time really goes and how much of it you can easily divert to your goal.

Call to action

Give your all. Leave it on the field every day and with every opportunity. Put in the work day-in and day-out. The results will begin to slowly sprout and blossom. Eventually, you'll feel as if you're living another life.

Knowing that it's going to take work will help prevent feelings of despair or inadequacy that might make you feel like grabbing a bag of chips and settling in on the couch for a marathon TV session.

Knowing others have discovered a better life when they discovered their passion is inspiring. Let this knowledge give you that extra and often-need motivation to take another step towards your passion and GREATNESS.

What does this mean for you?

_____

_____

_____

_____

_____

PURE BELIEF IN YOURSELF

By now, you've learned about your unlimited potential, the true calling of your soul, and your passion. Those three things are powerful and life changing, but you also must believe in yourself.

It's important to remember there is nothing you can't do. At times, the only person to believe in your dream or goals will be you. And as your only cheerleader, it's vital to always keep your inner voice in top form. Regularly remind yourself that yes, you can accomplish anything.

To keep away the gloom and doom, try posting notes around the house (next to the bed, on the fridge, on the bathroom mirror, and anywhere else you might see them frequently throughout the day). Consider the following mantras:

- There is nothing I can't do.
- Anything is attainable.

- I will begin every day with a sense of purpose.

- My life is what I make it, and I will make it amazing.

- No one will stop me from my goals.

By reminding yourself that you are the only thing that stands in your way, it makes it easier to toss aside any doubts and stay focused on the win.

You need to keep your positive sides strong to block any negative energy coming from others. You know what you're capable of, and you know what you're committed to making happen, even if others don't.

Forget the haters

Face it. There will always be people who can't or won't give you the confidence boost you're looking for. In fact, there are those who instead of being supportive would rather knock you down just so they can point and laugh at seeing you fall.

Those people, who seek out the worst in you and are quick to point out your faults, do so because they aren't like you. They don't have your skill set, confidence, ability, or perseverance. They will always be on the losing team, and deep down, they hate it there. Being a loser has made them bitter and angry. And really, who can blame them?

[38]

Frankly, if you don't have haters, then you're dreams probably aren't big enough. When people are telling you "no" and "you can't," that's a good indicator you're on the right path towards something big. Haters love misery and misery loves company. The haters want you to stay in the land of mediocrity and keep them company as they go nowhere. Instead of getting irritated by the naysayers and their negativity, simply smile inside knowing that their pessimism means you're dreams are big enough and you're going places.

Forget what they have to say and walk away. Just be sure to wave as you're leaving them behind in a cloud of dust. It's been said time and time again, "The best revenge is massive success." Ignore the haters and focus on succeeding.

Alone again, naturally

Leaders often stand alone.

Barack Obama faced a wealth of opposition before becoming the first African-American President of the United States. Many pundits said the nation wasn't ready for a Black President and were quick to point out that Obama was wasting his time.

But he believed that his message of hope and change was one that America was ready for. He didn't give up, even when his poll numbers were low and everyone expected the McCain-Palin ticket to win.

He approached the presidency with a sense of belief in himself that never wavered. It began when he chose to make his bid for the Democratic nomination in the Illinois city of Springfield. Choosing the former home of Abraham Lincoln and the symbolic gesture of channeling the iconic president wasn't missed by Obama supporters. In fact, it likely sealed his win.

And now, with a health care plan in place and other programs coming down the pipeline, Obama is poised to do it all over again, leaving behind the naysayers in the process.

When eying a goal that seems larger than life, you have to expect some people to say it will never happen. And when you're told you aren't going to be a success, make it your mission to prove the naysayers wrong.

Call to action

Believe in yourself. Ignore the haters, naysayers, and critics.

Only you know what you can do. If you say you can do it, then that's all there is too it. That's it. You have the final word. The decision is yours and yours alone.

Your belief in yourself will often be like a life vest keeping you buoyant during turbulent times and troubled waters. Your belief in yourself will often carry you or push you through those pivotal periods on which defeat or success hinge. Believe in yourself.

What does this mean for you?

_____

_____

_____

_____

_____

SEEK THOSE WHO PAVED THE WAY

Even though many leaders might stand alone in their success, they didn't claw their way to the top all by themselves.

Even Donald Trump had the helping hand of his father's business and business acumen to get where he was going. He didn't do it alone.

Reach out...

Remember, it's okay to ask for a helping hand along the way. Choose someone you know will offer sage advice about how to avoid the sacks and get into the end zone without being tackled.

Finding a coach and mentor is a great first step. People who have already walked a road you want to travel have ideas on how to bypass the pitfalls.

They've fallen and gotten back up again. They've been in your shoes. Let their success be your guide.

Find someone to model

One of the key pieces of advice from self-help guru Anthony Robbins is to copy your idols; doing exactly what they do to get the same results.

By modeling yourself after someone who has what you want, you'll be a step ahead of everyone else; especially those who decide to forge their own path without a clue about how to get to the finish line.

Swallow your pride

Make sure you don't let your pride and your need to stand alone get in the way of asking someone else for assistance. The saying "pride goes before a fall" is one that came about for a reason.

Admitting that others might know more than you do is a sure sign that you're smart enough to know what to do under any circumstances. Everyone needs help at one time or another and successful people know that. They've used the success of others as their guide.

Call to action

It's OK to ask for help. Mentors and models are great resources. Simply swallow your pride and ask for advice, help, or suggestions.

- If you want to be an actor, audition for a local show. Find someone there who is willing to give you tips on how you can improve your stage presence.

- If your goals involve landing a spot as an exec at a local company, snag a job as an intern first. Offer to work for free and keep your eyes open while you're there to glean all you can from those around you.

- If you want your boss's job, watch him or her work, and do what he or she does.

What does this mean for you?

_____

_____

_____

_____

_____

WHAT WILL MAKE IT WORTH IT FOR YOU?

"Without visions and dreams, life is pretty empty and quiet."

Sometimes, even with your goals in place and mentors lined up, you still need a little nudge to get started, no matter what your mission in life.

And although your desires might be clear and the end zone is clearly in focus, sometimes it's hard to get there without a strong driving force to move you along the way. That's why you must discover *what will make it worth it for you?*

Your reasons for doing

Knowing the real reasons your goal manifested itself is vital to determining what will make it worth it for you.

Are you looking to become a business mogul a la Donald Trump so that you have money to donate to your favorite local charity? Or are you inclined to start a new business so your family will be secure long after you are

[45]

gone? Whatever the reasons, here's where getting a close-up look at your motivation is vital to success.

The reasons for your goals are valuable sources of energy that you'll need to carry you when you feel as if you have nothing left to give. Your reasons will help you focus and concentrate on what matters. Life is full of distractions – all of them jockeying for your priceless time and attention.

I can see clearly now

Here are two ways to see the true worth of your desire.

1. **Volunteer** - Start volunteering at a local charity or the business where you hope to donate funds. Seeing those in need of your assistance will help keep you motivated.

2. **Connect with Models** - Notice how those you respect and admire interact with their families. Use what you see to help you spend more quality time with yours. By knowing your family's dreams and aspirations, you'll have a better sense of why you want to do right by them.

No pain, no gain

Remember that any long-term goal is worth the pain you experience at the beginning of the journey.

When athletes and Olympians feel pain, they welcome it. They know the type of pain their experiencing is what's necessary to prepare them for victory. Likewise, the pains you might periodically feel along the way are simply the necessary stimulus to help you grow into a person of GREATNESS.

Give a little bit

What makes it worth it for many people is someone else. Having a goal of making a difference in someone else's life is a great motivator. There's a bit of altruist in everyone. Finding yours will make all the difference.

Now at the peak of their careers, Jay-Z and his wife Beyonce are involved with multiple charities, from ensuring fresh water for the people of Angola to providing musical instruments and even a concert appearance to the Mesa Arts Academy for students in need.

Also, they know that in order to be able to give to others, they have to maintain their places in the music industry. They cannot do one without the other. Jay-Z and Beyonce must feel really good to be in a position to make a difference in the lives of others.

Giving is what helps pave the way for the heavy lifting required by your dream. This doesn't have to be a reason for your dream, but if it is, know that is a very strong one.

What will make it worth it for you? Ask yourself that question. Write down everything that comes to mind. It's not for others to judge what matters to you. That's your unique privilege, opportunity, and choice. Also, don't be too critical of yourself. Don't think that your reasons are silly. If they make it worth it for you, they're not silly. They're necessary.

Call to action

For every success story, there are at least one-thousand "almost" success stories.

Knowing your reasons will carry you from the realms of "almost" successful to actually successful. Your reasons will make you relentless in the face of fatigue, financial problems, or family issues. Your reasons "why" will be so big and pulsating that you'll have no choice but to keep moving toward your goal regardless of what's taking place in your environment or your life.

Whatever you do, don't let another day go by without writing a long list of reasons why you "must" turn your dream into a reality. Remember, you can never have too many reasons, but you can have too few.

What will make it worth it for you?

How does this affect you?

_____

_____

_____

_____

_____

ALL IN

"Success is what you make it, so go make it."

You can't sit on the sidelines, waiting for someone else to give you the go-ahead to get in the game. You have to be "all in." You must be fully invested in order to make it happen. You know what you want and why you want it. Now, it's time to go get it.

Time to Produce

Making your dream happen by being *all in* requires an investment of your time. You don't want to become an *all work and no play* kind of person, but you can't expect dreams to happen while you're lounging around in your underwear watching "Sports Center."

You have to **get in the game,** not just watch it play out around you.

No looking back

Kick those old doubts to the curb right now. The past has passed, what's done is done. There is only the future, and yours will be so bright, you'll have to wear shades.

Your days of waiting for something to happen are over, and now it's time to suit up and get out there.

Commit to the end

Bryant Young didn't let the end of his pro football career kick him out of the game.

After more than a decade as one of the nation's top players – he helped lead the San Francisco 49ers to Super Bowl victory in 1994 – Young retired from the game.

He could have gone home and put his feet up. But he didn't, because football was in his blood. And within a few years, he landed a gig coaching for his alma mater, Notre Dame. He currently serves as the defensive line coach for the University of Florida Gators.

He is 100 percent vested in his life as a football legend, and he didn't stop at halftime. He plans to stay in the game until the end.

Call to action

Get in the game. Live your life. Make your dreams happen.

If it all seems overwhelming, break it down and tackle a little bit at a time.

1. Spend 15 minutes a day on the tough stuff. Even if tackling some project on your list seems impossible, know that you can spend at least 15 minutes a day doing almost anything. After enough time has passed, the project that seemed unimaginable is done, in just minutes a day.

2. Keep the ultimate goal clearly in focus, not just in the abstract. Write it down and refer to it regularly.

3. Start small. It can only get bigger from here.

How does this affect you?

_____

_____

_____

_____

_____

2nd Quarter

"Never keep your head down. Always look up so you can see when your next blessing is coming."

2nd Down: Action

"Why talk about what you will do? Just do it and let everyone else talk."

There can be no form of change, regardless of how big or small, without some type of action. Let's say for example you desire to lose weight! What steps would you need to go through physically, mentally, and emotionally? What if the goal was to lose 20 pounds in 4 months? How might you tackle that goal? What type of support would you need? Who would you like to have in your corner? Where would you get the information from to start the journey?

Whatever your desire, always remember that *some form of action must be present.* While it's always great to recruit external resources and the help of others, there's simply only one person who must take action. You!

One-hundred percent of the work has to be done by you. There is no way around that. In fact, it's better that way. *No matter what the cause, you have to be willing to do all the work.* There is no other person on this planet that can lose the 20 pounds for you. If you desire to learn a new language, say Spanish, without a doubt the work has to be done by you. Let this principle sink deep within you. This principle is what separates boys from men and girls from women. Applying this principle will transform your vision into a reality.

The simplest way to gain confidence when it comes to action is to follow the footsteps of Jack Canfield and Mark Victor Hansen. Jack and Mark were the creators of the wildly popular and successful book series, "Chicken Soup for the Soul." Their message was *do three things towards your goal every day.*

Taking action does not have to be a dreaded process that makes you feel tired, worn out, and scared before you've even started. Begin by doing something little every day. Let's go back to that goal of losing 20 pounds. Start by taking two or three small tasks each day until you've built up the confidence and steam to accomplish more. Perhaps you decide that on Wednesdays you will walk two laps around the track, eat a salad for lunch, and do Zumba in the evenings. Those are three pivotal action steps that can lead to success without making you feel overwhelmed, stressed, and de-motivated.

Confucius said, "When it is obvious that the goals cannot be reached don't adjust the goals, adjust the action steps." That really sums it up. How powerful is that?! It is time for you to begin taking action steps towards your desire. The road won't be easy; nevertheless, you'll make excellent progress by being committed to your plans. Accomplish a little every day, one step at a time.

Good Luck and Commit to GREATNESS!!!

[56]

MASSIVE WORK ETHIC

"There comes a time when you must say enough is enough. Because there can be no circumstance that keeps you from destiny."

Knowing you'll be fully vested in your mission will allow you to make the most of every day.

Stay inspired by remembering that every moment you work toward you goal brings it closer to fruition. With perseverance you can move mountains, even if you only do it one grain of sand at a time.

Unleash your inner beast

Be the best you can be, every day.

Consider the life of late football superstar Reggie White. He was known throughout the NFL as the Minister of Defense because he didn't stop at being one of the most celebrated players in the NFL. He also was an ordained minister for the Inner City Church in Knoxville, Tennessee. White used his fame to draw attention to his community's needs.

[57]

He always gave his all to his projects and had a work ethic that made him completely beloved throughout the NFL.

White died only four years after retiring from the NFL, following stints with the Green Bay Packers, Carolina Panthers, and Philadelphia Eagles, yet, his name lives on. His is the voice at the sleep apnea center, which was founded by his wife to continue his legacy of helping others. The center helps people overcome the potentially fatal sleep disorder that played a pivotal role in White's death.

Even now, White continues to make a difference in people's lives every day, and you can, too, even if you're not a pro football player. His work ethic lives on, and with the right effort and investment, so can yours.

Leave it on the field

Keep in mind that engaging in dissention or conflict with your team, whether at work or at home, only distracts you from your goals.

So forget the petty squabbles, toss aside the arguments about who did what, and always accept responsibility if you make a mistake.

Whatever happens, be a real man or a real woman and own it. And then move on. Don't waste a second on blame, anger, bitterness, or vengefulness.

Like regret, these types of feelings or thoughts, just detract from your true goals.

Be the first one to arrive, the last one to leave

Those people who get the great jobs or huge promotions are the ones who are working for them.

They don't rely on their connections to get them there, but their reputations. The guy who wins in the long run isn't sleeping at his desk, watching the clock for quitting time, or sneaking in late morning after morning.

If that's you, get a new job, because the one you have doesn't inspire your passion. If it did, you'd be the first one to arrive and the last one to leave.

And that's the guy who's going places.

Developing your work ethic

At this point, you probably understand that a committed "work ethic" is a prerequisite to your success. Unfortunately, too many people make the mistake of believing they'll work harder *after* they become successful and consequently never achieve their goals. A strong work ethic doesn't follow GREATNESS, it leads and precedes GREATNESS.

The point is you must put in the work right now. You must give it your all, not only today but every day, until your dream is realized.

Call to action

So, what can someone do who lacks a solid work ethic?

1. Look at your daily routines and find a task or responsibility you often overlook or simply don't do well. If you find yourself stumped, then just ask a family member, spouse, or loved one to point out something you consistently do that needs improvement. (I'm sure they'll be able to give you a few examples.)

2. Armed with just one task or activity, reflect on what you can do to make the activity consistent, excellent, or enjoyable.

3. Write down all of your ideas, keeping each one to a few sentences at most. Choose one or two of those ideas and assign an ideal time to do each one. For example, if you decide you want to improve the consistency or frequency with which you workout each week, then one idea might be to prepare your gym bag or workout gear immediately after you finish a workout. This is one way many fitness veterans keep themselves ready to go for the next workout or even an extra workout.

4. Commit to and execute each item on your list using the idea or ideas you developed in step 3. Do this for 7 to 10 consecutive days. Make sure your "improvement task or activity" only has one

or two daily action items. Having more than that can be overwhelming and could result in procrastination. Having just one or two, however, can result in a major change.

5. After you've successfully completed the action item(s) every day for 7 to 10 days, continue to do that action item (s) and then add more as you feel comfortable.

A work ethic isn't developed in a few days, but becomes stronger and more automatic as you consistently improve various actions, tasks, or habits. It's like getting to work on time, which many people struggle to do with consistency.

Even more perplexing is the fact the job, which they're always late for, is most people's sole source of income. Furthermore, most people are living check to check, yet still aren't hungry enough or serious enough about improving their financial situation, to simply show up to work on time.

If this sounds like you, make this your "work ethic improvement" task as it's an excellent one that definitely has big benefits for you.

The great news is that any person can take his or her flabby work ethic and transform it into the work ethic of

GREATNESS. It only takes your commitment to improve your work ethic, one step at a time.

How does this affect you?

_____

_____

_____

_____

_____

YOU ARE SUPPOSED TO BE HERE

"Your biggest obstacle is not believing in yourself."

If you're putting in the effort to make it happen, you deserve to reap the rewards that come your way.

And no matter what advantages others had in life to get where they are – old money, a family with a great reputation in town, or benefactors with deep pockets – they are certainly not more deserving than you are.

Even if it seems impossible, remember that others also fought their way to the top, so you can do it too.

Get tough about it, and you'll notice the world and people will come to the aid of your dreams. Things will eventually begin to fall into place for you.

His was not a small world

When Walt Disney passed away in the early 1960s, he died a legend, unforgettable in America thanks to movies, theme parks, and memorabilia.

But that doesn't mean he was without his own forms of self-doubt. His first dream was to become a political cartoonist, but newspapers didn't want him. He then developed an interest in animation working at an ad company, but soon found himself battling to recover after losing one of his first characters, Oswald the Rabbit, in a contract dispute.

The setbacks might have made Disney believe he had no place in the entertainment industry, but he used them to his advantage.

To replace Oswald, Mickey Mouse was born. Now Disney's most iconic character, Mickey was introduced in a short called "Steamboat Willie," and he soon became the country's most popular animated figure, overtaking the competing character Felix the Cat.

Won't be pigeonholed

There was nothing about Disney's early days that would have predicted his future. He had dropped out of school at the age of 16 and struggled to find his first job as an artist. Based on the misguided belief that everyone has a certain station in life, his life should have involved landing a job at the local jelly factory where his father worked.

But Disney had other ideas about what he wanted out of life. And in order to get there, he played up the following qualities:

- Perseverance
- Determination
- Adaptability
- Innovation

Despite going bankrupt as well as having a nervous breakdown, Disney didn't let setbacks stop him. He turned a single famous animated mouse into a media empire that now includes "Cinderella," "Snow White," "Alice in Wonderland," "The Little Mermaid," "The Artistocats," "Beauty and the Beast," and so many more.

Call to action

Take inspiration from Disney and remember that no matter where you came from, you too deserve success. And NOW is the time to go for it.

For many people, simply believing in themselves is the biggest obstacle to their dreams. Make the commitment today, from now and forever, to hold the mindset that you deserve and are supposed to achieve your dreams. After all, they are your dreams.

1. Be on the lookout for negative self-talk or negative people.

2. Any time a negative or doubtful thought passes through your mind, counter it silently or out loud by saying, "I deserve it and I'm supposed to have it."

3. Kindly correct anyone who decides to make a gloomy comment or pass judgment about your dream. Don't just sit there. Nicely let them know, "that's fine if you feel that way, but I'm going to do it because it's meant for me."

4. Hang around naysayers as infrequently as possible. The last thing you or your dreams need is to have a dark cloud always hanging around waiting to rain on your dreams.

How does this affect you?

_____

_____

_____

_____

_____

NO ACTION = NO RESULTS

The truth is only you can make your dreams come true.

As Newton's third Law of Motion clearly states, to every action there is an equal and opposite reaction. When you apply that to life, it essentially means that only by taking action can you get real results. It is insane to repeatedly do the same thing over and over again and expect a different result. No action equals no results. Your life will not change, you're dreams will not be realized, and your GREATNESS will not be unleashed….until you take action.

Waiting around for someone else to do the work or foolishly playing games to run out the clock is not going to get the job done. No one can and no one will do the work for you.

Resist inertia

There's a reason why people feel even lazier after a day or two spent in front of the TV or napping. It's called inertia. An object at rest tends to stay at rest, while an object in motion tends to stay in motion.

Serious runners wake up ready for action, and many have their shoes tied before their feet officially hit the floor.

They know that to get results they have to get moving, and so they do every day.

Why continue drooling over the lean muscles of your neighbor's legs or the sleek car he drives? Hit the road and get what you want by putting in the effort yourself. Take action and achieve your desired results. Whether you need to take action in your financial life or your personal life, get busy.

Why settle for less?

People too often settle right in the middle. It's generally an area that's not too bad, but not too good either. It's a lukewarm environment where people are just maintaining a mediocre existence. They are treading water instead of actually swimming and moving in the direction of their choosing.

Sure, you can make do with running a few times a week, doing just enough to keep your heart healthy. But it

[70]

won't be enough to get the lean, sleek look of Kobe Bryant, who is a master of the basketball court, one of the stars of the Los Angeles Lakers, and a 2008 MVP.

Setting your goals higher can help you reach higher levels than you ever imagined.

And while Bryant's father, a now retired pro basketball player, might have encouraged his son to follow in his footsteps and set the stage for his success, Bryant still had to do the work to get to the Lakers stadium. It was 100 percent him. He alone took the steps to make his dreams come true, even though the hours he spent training every day was tough.

Call to action

To get through the tough stuff, take one extra step, make one extra move, to prove to yourself that you can do it.

Only then will you be able to sit back and reap the rewards of your efforts.

So go for it. The only one stopping you is you. Don't allow yourself to be stuck to the leather of your Lazy Boy, watching Kobe play. Instead, you need to get in the game. Live your dreams.

1. Write down one action you can take every day that will move you closer to your goals.

2. Consistently take that action until it becomes automatic.

3. Identify another singular action that will move you towards your goals.

4. Repeat steps 2 and 3 until you achieve your goal.

There's a lot of power in simply taking one step or action towards your goal every day. Results begin appearing, and before you know it, you're where you always believed you were supposed to be – living your dreams.

How does this affect you?

_____

_____

_____

_____

_____

THE MIRROR OF POSITIVE AFFIRMATION

While Stuart Smalley might have been considered a joke on "Saturday Night Live," the guy was right about one thing.

Positive affirmations are essential to ensuring you feel amazing and capable every day of your life.

They also help ensure that you don't end up like Chris Farley's "SNL" character Matt Foley. He was a motivational speaker who motivated others only by offering up a portrait of his own miserable life spent living in a van down by the river.

Tell yourself you can

Affirmations have a place in achieving your dreams. Self-help guru Anthony Robbins is all about unleashing the power within. He uses affirmations to remind clients they are able to accomplish anything they set their minds to. The key is to get rid of any self-doubt, and that's where affirmations come in.

[74]

Robbins has written two books, "Unlimited Power" and "Awaken the Giant Within," both of which focus on the idea that everyone is completely and totally capable of GREATNESS.

One of the goals of this book is to provide you with inspiring words and proven instructions to help you achieve your dreams.

I also hope that at least some of the words and information here serve as excellent daily affirmations for you.

Erase negativity

Negativity is like a curtain that blocks the sun. Erasing negativity opens the curtains – and provides a gateway to many good things.

So forget Negative Nelly (or to continue the "SNL" examples, Debbie Downer) and kick to the curb all those voices that suggest "you can't".

Replace the negativity with positive energy, and keep the following affirmations in your arsenal so you can haul them out when times are tough:

- Every day in every way, I am getting better and better.

- The past is gone. I live only in the present.

- I am a radiant being filled with light and love.

- My good comes from everywhere and everyone. All is well in my world.

Call to action

While on this earth, you have a responsibility to yourself and to the universe to make the most of your life.

So accept Robbins' challenge and "make your life a masterpiece."

As Robbins has said, "If you do what you've always done, you'll get what you've always gotten."

That means that the only thing stopping you from success is you. So get out of the way. Realize that you are capable and amazing and tell yourself that every day.

Do it now. Look in the mirror and tell yourself that right now, on this new and wonderful day, things are changing. And on this day, anything is possible.

What changes can you make today?

_____

_____

_____

_____

_____

YOU CAN ONLY WIN IF YOU PLAY

"If you have not reached your true potential, then "get off the sideline and get in the game." That is where winners are made."

Publishers Clearinghouse makes a good point with its slogan, "You can't win if you don't enter." That's also the way it is in life.

If you don't play, you can't take home the trophy. You have to get in the game to win.

Los Angeles Dodgers outfielder Matt Kemp could have never landed on records lists alongside the legendary Hank Aaron if he had not grabbed his bat and taken a swing.

He got in the game in high school and put in the work he needed to rise to the top.

[78]

And you can do the same.

Stop settling
Sure, the field is packed with other players and competitors.

But those at the top were once where you are now, and they made it. They weren't wasting time worrying about how hard it is to accomplish things. They took aim, targeting a successful future, and so should you.

So go ahead and claim the unattainable, because it's within reach. Your dreams don't have to be the carrot you can never grab because it's always just a bit out of your reach. You can attain any goal if you become a player instead of a spectator.

Forget the blame game
Some people spend time taking aim at others for their own lack of success. The truth is, they really only have themselves to blame. Mayme White Miller wrote a poem that Ben Carson, famed neurosurgeon at the world-renowned Johns Hopkins Hospital, found very influential as he was growing up. Dr. Carson actually learned the poem from his mother who had memorized it; as Ben, himself, would later go on to do. The poem is called, "Yourself to Blame."

Yourself to Blame

by Mayme White Miller

If things go bad for you
And make you a bit ashamed
Often you will find out that
You have yourself to blame

Swiftly we ran to mischief
And then the bad luck came
Why do we fault others?
We have ourselves to blame

Whatever happens to us,
Here is what we say
"Had it not been for so-and-so
Things wouldn't have gone that way."

And if you are short of friends,
I'll tell you what to do
Make an examination,
You'll find the faults in you...

You're the captain of your ship,
So agree with the same
If you travel downward
You have yourself to blame

[80]

You are responsible for not only your successes, but also your failures. Accepting that can put those failures into a better perspective, allowing you to move on and win.

Get off the sidelines

Many people find themselves sitting around watching other people who are landing the great jobs or getting the great girls or guys. But dreaming about it won't make it happen.

Your life won't change unless you change. It's up to you to take the bull by the horns and harness your potential.

Don't be one of those folks who pretend to be content with their life as it is, but inwardly wish they had more, did more, and felt like more.

It's time to stop the lie and admit when you're not happy. Only then will you have the motivation and realistic perspective that will pull you from the sidelines and into the game.

Call to action

Make a firm commitment that beginning right now, you're going to get in the game. Get off the sidelines and play to win.

Remember that the time for your name to be in lights is coming. It's a waste of time to hang out at the bottom. There's no elbowroom.

Start playing today so you can rise to the top, where there's a lot more space to move around and a better view.

What changes can you make today?

_____

_____

_____

_____

_____

3rd Quarter

"If you dream too small, you just might achieve it. If you dream too big, you just might achieve it. So, which one shall you choose?"

Third Down: Struggle

"Just because you decide to get out of bed does not mean you will win the war of life."

Willie Jolley, of whom I am a huge fan, said, "Life and Flight are in the struggle." This statement is fitting for most people throughout the world. What does it mean? In a nutshell, it means *before you can prosper or become successful in life you have to experience struggle.*

Without the experience of struggle, you can't really know what you're made of. How can you find, discover, or embrace your true character unless you have been knocked down by life? You weren't put on this planet to be average or mediocre. However, *you sometimes need your back against the wall* to break free of the chains of mediocrity, realize your true strength and potential, *and* unleash your inner-power that has been there all along.

Once you have gone through a struggle, you tend to have a clearer mind as well as the newfound knowledge of what steps are needed for you to win the race. *The struggle is not the end; it's the beginning of success.*

When you have fought hard for something and then your plan goes astray, that just means you need to make a few adjustments to keep it on course. Take a moment and think about some of the most successful people you know. I bet that somewhere in their life they've failed. Nevertheless, *the key is they did not stop.* It's important to understand that in life some investments, ideas, and businesses just won't work. However, as long as you keep playing in the game, eventually you will prosper because you have made up your mind that there is just no other way.

Think of a time when you were fighting an uphill battle. How did you handle it? What did you learn from it? More importantly, how did you come through it? No matter how big or small the hurdle was it was still a hurdle. Throughout your life you have been knocked down numerous times, but you have still found a way to prevail.

All I ask now is that you *find what is burning inside of you.* What do you aspire to be, do, or have? Now is the time for you to prepare to reach your dreams and goals at whatever the cost.

Fredrick Douglas said, *"If there is no struggle there is no progress."* You can fight through any struggle. You have been doing it your whole life. Now it's time to up the stakes to achieve your GREATNESS. The time is now.

Good Luck and Be Great!!!

[86]

AVERAGE WILL ALWAYS BE AVERAGE

Sure, it hurts a little bit to break out of the mold. Even after you decide to play and get in the game, there's that sinister temptation, to which many people fall victim, to just be average.

Remind yourself you aren't in the game to be average. You're in the game and you're playing to win. Challenge yourself a little bit harder.

Remember that others around you might criticize you or mock you for taking a chance. However, never forget that their negativity is only their own fears talking. They only take pot shots at you because they aren't brave enough to make the same moves. Haters are only an indication you're headed in the right direction.

Shoot for the stars

When Denzel Washington landed the role of Grapes in the classic Fruit of the Loom commercials, he could have been satisfied with that average bit of TV exposure. And maybe his friends and family told him he should be satisfied. It was national exposure, after all.

Instead of settling, he leveraged his undergarment gig first into a TV movie and later, into his groundbreaking role on the Emmy-winning medical drama "St. Elsewhere."

That star-making turn led to a wealth of movie roles that catapulted him from TV actor to Golden Globe winner. In 2000, he took home the award for best actor in a drama, becoming the second African-American to earn the award, bested only by Sidney Poitier.

God didn't mean for anyone to be average

God made each person in his own image, and that means everyone is amazing.

Not average. Amazing!

The status quo might be all right for some people, but certainly not for you. Being average isn't living up to God's potential for you.

Call to action

Keep the words of Joel Osteen in your head every day. The popular television evangelist shares his own personal challenges, along with those of others, to help his congregation be their own personal best. "That best is something God expects for all of us," Joel says in almost every sermon. He also says, "Although you may not be where you want to be yet, you're on your way, and that is what matters."

People are born for GREATNESS. And that means you. Average will always be average. So bid adios to average. That's for someone else.

What changes can you make today?

_____

_____

_____

_____

_____

YOU CAN'T AFFORD NOT TO

Look around you for a minute. How many of the people that you see every day have lives that are simply average?

Are they happy with that? Would you be happy with that? You shouldn't be. You know that you were born to be more than average, right? And that doesn't mean a permanent gig at your local 7-11 store, no matter how good the employee discount.

Besides, if you don't fulfill your true potential, you'll hate yourself and you'll hate your life. And how is being filled with hatred a healthy way to wake up every morning?

Not reaching for the stars will lead to decay in your life that could make you turn to unhealthy things or counterproductive activities to numb the pain of failure.

You can't afford not to get in the game and unleash your GREATNESS. The price and consequences for not doing so are simply too painful.

Fear is unacceptable

Staying the course because you're afraid to make changes is foolhardy at best. It will leave you stagnating in a pool of dissatisfaction.

Sure, you're afraid. Change is always a little bit scary.

But you're flexible and built for change. So laugh your fear in the face and go for it. There's only one shot at this life. Don't waste it.

Fear is an unacceptable reason for not taking action. If you can't banish your fear, then drag it along as you move towards your dreams. Never let fear stop you.

Call to action

If the course of your life is going in the wrong direction, you can change it before things get out of hand.

All you need to do is give yourself a good halftime pep talk and get back in the game.

- Set a deadline to quit the job you despise.

- Make calls to the heads of businesses where you want to work.

- Don't give up. Others will recognize your strength and determination.

- Keep your sense of humor along the way.

Former college and pro football coach Lou Holtz used humor to inspire players while in the locker room. This is something you can do as well.

Laugh at the wrong moves you've made so far and use any mistakes to lead you in the right direction.

You can't afford not to take the steps and make the changes necessary to unleash life's best for you. Get in the game!

What changes can you make today?

_____

_____

_____

_____

_____

ENJOY THE JOURNEY

Your success and GREATNESS depends on many things. Dreaming, believing, setting goals, taking action, never settling, and remaining positive are all important. However, the final component is the most important one and often overlooked by people.

Believe it or not, you can get all of the other success elements right, yet only come in second place if you leave out the last ingredient. Remember, second place is the first place to lose. I am sure that is not what you want.

Not only will this final ingredient be of great benefit, you will definitely be glad to learn it. However, before you read about this final detail, let's discuss the significance of bad seasons in your life.

Every aspect of your life fulfills a purpose

Life is truly an extraordinary experience. There are so many different seasons. Some are good and some are not so good. It can sometimes be difficult to believe every aspect of this; especially that the not so good seasons or experiences are there for positive reasons. The truth is you learn from both the good and the bad seasons. Both are extremely beneficial.

Look at today's economy. There are people facing serious hardships. It may be a family struggling to pay their mortgage or a business owner trying to make payroll. The lessons learned during these times are all valuable ones. When you successfully fight through those challenges, you develop into a stronger person.

Whatever doesn't kill you makes you stronger. I firmly believe that. There are many opportunities to learn from the negative experiences in your life. These lessons will prepare and strengthen you for similar circumstances in the future. A problem is not a problem for the man or woman who is prepared. Your previous challenges and difficulties prepare you to handle new obstacles with ease when they arise. Furthermore, they build character, discipline, and skills beneficial to the other dimensions of your life. Trials and problems you overcome build your confidence. If you have done it before, you can do it again. Therefore, I truly believe you learn from both the positive and negative experiences in life.

Take the position or posture of a student of life. Have an open mind and humble spirit, accepting that you do not know it all. Understand that when things do not work out exactly as you want, you can still have what you desire and reach your dreams.

I have heard it said, "A setback is nothing more than a setup for a comeback." View your setbacks as an opportunity to provide you with the information and experience to be victorious on the next attempt.

Study any successful athlete, entrepreneur, or person. Do not just look at their present results, fame, wealth, and glory. Dig deep and search for what happened before their success. You will undoubtedly find that almost every one of them experienced great challenges. The world is full of people who are the best at what they do, yet these same people faced adversities that stop most people dead in their tracks. Successful people take lemons, make lemonade, sell it for a profit, and enjoy life. They make it happen. You can too.

Billion dollar lessons

You would think that a billionaire would know it all...at least as far as money or business was concerned, right? Wrong! Donald Trump amassed a fortune of over a billion dollars and lost it all. Most people find that part of the story very remarkable. I do not. People lose money and fortunes all the time. What inspires me and piques my interest is the next part.

A billion dollars is a lot to lose. Many people cannot fathom the loss of $1,000 or $100,000, not to mention

$1,000,000. Trump lost over $1,000,000,000! That's one billion dollars! How many millions are in a billion? One-thousand! He lost a fortune! One thousand million dollars...gone!

OK, so here's the sweet part. Are you ready for this? He earned it all back again! That is miraculous. That is inspirational. The next time you are wondering whether you can recover from your financial or other losses, remember Trump. If he can recoup one billion dollars, then you can surely recoup whatever you have lost.

Do not bury your head in the sand when problems come your way. Trump did not. He learned from his mistakes and adversities. You too must examine the mistakes or wrong choices you have made in order to avoid any such future difficulties. Once you have done that, you can take your newly discovered wisdom and give it another go. Success is waiting for you!

It's not fair

OK, I left out a very real and common issue regarding life's difficult little gifts. Fairness. What if you did not do anything wrong? What if you did not make a mistake? Unfortunately, misfortune and bad events will occasionally fall upon you regardless of your actions. It happens. Let's borrow a lesson from the game of basketball that can help you overcome unfair difficulties with massive success.

[97]

In addition to football, I am a basketball fan. I love the Los Angeles Lakers and think Kobe Bryant is a phenomenal basketball player. While watching "Doing Work," a Spike Lee documentary of Kobe Bryant, I was quite impressed and amazed by Kobe's wisdom. He is the captain of his team, therefore, he not only has the pressure of delivering a stellar performance every game, but he must also lead and coach his teammates.

Sitting on the bench, one of Kobe's teammates began complaining about the referees failing to call the repeated fouls of a particular player on the opposing team, the San Antonio Spurs. Kobe's sharp reply redirected his teammate's energy and focus. "You have to play through it, that's all. Do not pay attention to that. It might happen all game. Just play through it, OK?" By the way, the Lakers won the game.

You too have to play through the things in life that are not fair. Take your mind off what is not going right and refocus on your goal. Play through it! It is easy to get caught up in the act of complaining. Unfortunately, life is not always fair, but you can still be great.

Do not let fairness determine whether you are victorious or not. Do not wait for life to give you your "fair share." You must develop the mindset and attitude that I deserve it, it is mine, and no one or nothing will deny me! Play through it and win.

[98]

The difference between champions, like Kobe, and others is that champions play through it and make it happen. Sometimes life will be fair and give you your due. Whenever it does not, make it happen for yourself. There is no circumstance or adversity capable of stopping you. Yes, something might slow you down or get in the way. What must you do? Regroup and go around, under, through, or over it! Make life and all of its circumstances serve you.

Enjoy the journey

Like anyone that wants to be successful there are still dreams and goals that I want to hit and that I will hit because I believe in my ability. The lessons I learn tonight and tomorrow will help me in my quest. They will help me in my journey.

The people I meet today, tomorrow, next week, next month, in six months...those people will help me in my quest. However, if I just let life go by in a blur, what experiences will I talk about when I achieve my quest? What experiences will I be able to share with someone else who has the same goals and dreams?

The experiences you have on your journey are what shape you. They create who you are. If you just let them go and do not really take anything from them, you will have done yourself a disservice.

As humans, we all struggle, everyone struggles with something. For me, enjoying the journey was one of the things I always struggled with because I wanted to achieve all my goals today. I did not want them to happen tomorrow or in six months. I wanted them right now.

I have learned in my journey from A to Z, that we have many different types of experiences. There are so many people we meet, some good and some bad. You have to run the course and as you keep going, fighting to reach your goals and dreams, you are going to meet wonderful people and have great experiences.

Life is short. You know that, right? Make the most out of everything you do and of the experiences along the way. That is the best choice. That is the final ingredient.

Sometimes you are not happy with the pursuit of your goals. You might have told yourself, 'I won't be happy until I get my law degree' (or whatever the goal). It is sad when you set your mind to be unhappy while pursuing a dream. In all likelihood, the pursuit and attainment of the goal will become harder because you are unhappy along the journey. Be happy during the journey. Enjoy it.

Understand that for you to be actively making progress towards your dreams and goals is a blessing. Realize that the time clock of life does not stop while you are on your

[100]

journey. The days, months, and years you overlook while pursuing your dream cannot be magically added back to your life later. So, enjoy each day, month, and year while you are on your way.

Call to action

'It's hard to be happy and content because I'm hard at work chasing my dreams while my friends are having fun.' Many people have that erroneous thought. It has crossed my mind a few times too. This concern is not unusual; however, it is unnecessary. Remember, that the reason you are pursuing your dream or goal and making sacrifices is to achieve something greater than you currently have in your life.

You might be working to provide a better life for your family, children, people in the community, or society in general, or you might be working so you can become financially independent and experience a better quality of life. Whatever it is, it is worth it.

I believe when you are earning, attaining, or pursuing something of greater value or significance than you currently possess – there really is no sacrifice. At the very least, if it is a sacrifice, then it is an excellent one! Give up the mediocre to go for the great. Know that while you are on your journey it is a path you must take in order to achieve GREATNESS.

After achieving a number of dreams and goals, I looked back at the many sacrifices I made in life and realized I did not lose or miss out on anything. Instead, I improved my life.

[102]

The journey you are on or about to set out on is and will be a blessing. Enjoy every moment of it!

What changes can you make today?

_____

_____

_____

_____

_____

MAKE QUITTING A NON-OPTION

Sure, life is hard. You know that. If it were easy, it wouldn't be worth it, anyway. Typically, it's the things you work for that matter most.

Difficult moments in life and hard work can sometimes summon an insidious urge to quit, even in the best of people. However, the difference between successful people and average people is quitting.

If you are serious about becoming great and living your dream every day, then you must do what successful people do - make quitting a non-option.

Always a quitter?

Things don't always go as planned. After all "the best laid plans of mice and men often go awry." If you always give up when things don't go according to plan, then you'll always be a quitter. Always quitting is a recipe for disaster – not success.

Sometimes, no matter how much you deserve it, the other guy gets the break. Nevertheless, giving up makes it impossible for you to finish the game or reach your goal. To throw in the towel is to reject the idea that you can accomplish your mission.

No doubt Ice Cube expected his stint with N.W.A. to last longer, given his contributions to the controversial group who altered the direction of music. But the music industry is a tough one, and his time with the band ended when he and his manager couldn't come to an agreement about money. He believed he was worth more, and he was willing to take a stand, even if it meant standing alone.

Ice Cube didn't quit. He turned his music career into a media empire that now includes a hot TV sitcom portraying him as a family man.

Easy does it?

Sure, the TV gig is probably unexpected for a guy who started out on the streets of L.A.'s Compton neighborhood; a tough part of the city where being the victim of a gang-related drive-by shooting is more likely than achieving any kind of success.

But Ice Cube used his hardships to his advantage. He didn't take the easy way out by quitting. Instead, he held his head high and got busy charting a new path, inspired by where he had been so far. It's how someone handles challenges that make them who they are. This is what leads people down the road to either success or failure.

Call to action

Make your vision clear to yourself. Make it known to those your trust, so you don't have the opportunity to get discouraged.

- Write down your desires.
- Make sure everyone around you knows your plans, so they can call you on them if you start to waver.
- Take simple steps every day to make things happen.

Remember, it will be difficult to quit knowing that if you do your friends and family will be around to hassle you for years to come. They, like elephants, will never forget. And they won't let you forget, either.

How does this apply to your life?

_____

_____

_____

_____

_____

BE A RAIDER & COMMIT TO EXCELLENCE

"Nothing in life is free. You must be willing to earn your way."

With three Super Bowl wins under their belts, players on the Oakland Raiders pro football team play to win.

Basing each game on their team motto, "commitment to excellence" is something that follows that the players take seriously. They follow that motto both on and off the field.

Under the 10 year tutelage of head coach and football legend John Madden, the team saw numerous Super Bowl bids as well as 13 former members inducted into the Football Hall of Fame.

A little bit of excellence every day

Take steps every day to make your goals come to fruition. It's a great way to keep your eye on the prize.

Making sure that everything you do is done well makes all the difference.

When you take pride in your actions and produce everything the best you can and the best it can be, you create a sense of purpose.

Whether you're making chef-worthy meals for your family or doing a home remodeling project, doing it to the best of your ability will instill a sense of accomplishment and pride, and that will follow you wherever you go.

Without aiming for excellence, what's the point, really? Doing something halfway with no passion only brings you down in other areas.

Determination in everything you do

For a football player, the mission starts the moment he awakens in the morning, when he begins fueling for the day with a protein-rich breakfast. The wrong choices here can foul things up later, so every move is essential.

That's what's at the heart of the Raiders' motto. Excellence in everything leads to excellence where it counts, particularly in your journey towards GREATNESS.

You get back what you put in. If you give garbage, you get garbage. So put in the best, every day. Make a commitment to yourself. Success is sure to follow.

Call to action

Target success. Here are four easily remembered ways you can target success and commit to excellence:

1. Set high standards for yourself.

2. Don't be content with mediocrity.

3. Don't stop until you win.

4. Make sure everyone around you is on board with the plan.

How does this apply to your life?

_____

_____

_____

_____

_____

4th Quarter

"To create a legacy you must be willing to sacrifice and endure."

Fourth Down: Success

"Successful people act it, know it, and believe it every day."

You've learned about vision, action, and struggle. Now you've finally reached the fourth and final key. It's all about success - your success.

We now live in an era when success can happen to anyone - a taxi driver, the corner dry cleaner, or a single-mom of three. *Success has no boundaries or limitations!*

Although success can land on anyone's doorstep, you must be willing to it seek it out. If you don't have a deep thirst for success, then it will steer clear of you. In other words, you have to fight, scratch, and claw to reach your desired success. Furthermore, you must be willing to *commit every day, good or bad, to a plan of action* that will allow success to seek you out.

There are many great and successful people in the world. The common themes among them are they:

- Did not listen to negative people
- Found a way to make it worth it
- Created a plan of action to stay the course
- Never ever gave up

[114]

Notice that I did not say great or successful people never fail, but rather they do not let failure stop them. You'll eventually come out on top if you commit to something for a long enough period of time.

Think about professional athletes and the commitment they have to their craft. The long days and nights they spend in the gym, the weight room, or on the track are simply to *gain an edge, even if it's a small one,* over the competition. Most people don't understand that *it won't be easy. Life is hard, but life is also forgiving if you are focused and persistent.*

The question I propose is 'will you have enough drive and strength to continue and to fight when it seems as though the world is against you?'

Success can be yours. It's possible for you to have the life or lifestyle of your desires. You have at least one thing in common with successful people including the likes of Oprah Winfrey, Bill Gates, and President Barack Obama. What's that one thing? The common theme between you, Oprah, Bill, and The President is that you are all human; you all put your pants on one leg at a time. This means there is no difference in your ability to *find something you are passionate about and devise a plan to pursue your dreams. Do that and you* are on the road to becoming just as successful as they are. The last step you need is to believe you can achieve your dreams.

[115]

Lack of belief and fear are what holds most people back, but I don't think you have to worry about that. I know you are driven. You are ready to change your life. I am proud of you.

Michael Jordan, arguably the best basketball player on the planet, put it this way, "I've failed over and over and over again in my life and that is why I succeed." It's time for you to go forth, live your dreams, and find your success!

Good Luck and Be Great!!!!

PERSISTENCE WINS

"Prosperity and abundance are not promised. But, a man's fight can lead him when hope seems dim."

When competing in a marathon, oftentimes runners hit the wall. It feels like it will be impossible for them to take one more step, no matter what the end result will be.

However, they push on. They push through the wall and their persistence wins the day. It is the same in the marathon of life. You have to push through those trouble spots. Your persistence will pay off!

Sure, you'll hit trouble spots. Pushing through those tough spots is where the choices come in. You can give up on your march to victory or you can stay the course and secure your GREATNESS. The latter choice is where dreamers are transformed into doers. Persistence transforms goals into achievements. Persistence wins.

The unstoppable will of Rice

NFL wide receiver Jerry Rice was on his way toward becoming one of the top players in football when a tackle by Warren Sapp during the first game of the San Francisco 49ers' season tore his knee ligaments in two places,

Here is where Rice's inner warrior came through, because he was back in the game in 14 weeks, scoring a touchdown that also lead to a fall that broke his kneecap in the process.

While the dual injuries would have sent many strong players to the sidelines, this was where Rice's inner warrior came through. He fought through the pain, and dug deep, yet again.

By the next season, Rice had made a full recovery. He was able to play almost another decade, earning the top spot on the 2010 list, "The Top 100: The NFL's Greatest Players" and a spot in the Pro Football Hall of Fame.

Call to action

At some point, just about everyone wants to give up. But if you do, you'll never get where you're going.

Rice only earned his titles with persistence and a mega-sized work ethic that led him to put in a little something extra every day so he could get that much closer to the goal post.

Stay the course and win. Let life find some other sucker to mess with.

How does this apply to your life?

_____

_____

_____

_____

_____

GOLDEN VISION FOR YOURSELF

"The key ingredient in setting goals is seeing yourself achieve them."

Gold medal-winning Olympic athletes don't spend a lot of time using the word *can't*.

Rather than thinking their dream of taking home the gold is impossible, they see it as not only totally possible, but also probable.

They know what their vision is and see it clearly enough to get them through even the toughest of days.

Their vision gives them the drive that makes it easier for them to get to the track or the pool every day, no matter the weather AND no matter how much they'd rather do something else.

[120]

To get where you want to go in life, it would be smart to borrow from the focused mindset and pure devotion of an Olympic athlete. Develop a golden vision for yourself.

What is your vision?

Do you know exactly what it is you want for your life? When you picture your future, do you see things clearly, or is the image distorted, as if you're seeing it while standing in front of a fun-house mirror?

Is your goal one that you feel strongly about? Is it something you want so badly you'll stop at nothing to achieve it?

That's the key component to most successful people. They see their golden vision and paint a vivid portrait in their mind. Then, they start tackling the things they need to accomplish in order to get there, checking them off the list one by one.

Set goals clearly

Athletes are great examples of successful people. As soon as they realize that their talents and drive can take them where they want to go, they set clear goals that can get them to the end zone with a championship ring or standing on the podium with their neck draped in gold, silver, or bronze.

And while you might have goals that are different than those of a professional athlete or Olympian, the road you travel will ultimately be the same.

And to make the trip successfully, you'll have to map out a path that will take you from start to finish. Make sure to include stepping stones along the way that can provide the successes you need for encouragement to take it all the way to the finish line.

Finding what drives you will help you best reach your goals, since you can't get to the finish without the fire to fuel you along the way.

Michael Phelps, who won a total of 22 medals in the 2004, 2008, and 2012 Olympic Games, more than any other athlete in history, realized his talents and drive early on. A diagnosis of attention-deficit hyperactivity disorder led his family to look for ways to help him drain his excess energy, and they decided on the pool.

At age 10, four years after he first jumped in the water, he had set a national record for his age group, and his future was set.

He continued to set records and win meets, turning his negatives into positives, and excelling despite his disability.

The pool changed his life.

[122]

Erasing the negatives

For you, recognizing those things that might hold you back and using them to your advantage is a smart way to get closer to your ultimate goal.

Are you a procrastinator? Experts now say that a little procrastination is a good thing. It is one of the key components pro athletes have that amateurs do not.

Frank Partnoy, author of the new book "Wait: The Art and Science of Delay," said that professional tennis players like Chris Evert may seem like they move faster than the amateurs do. They don't. Studies show that what they are really doing is delaying their shots by a few seconds more than their amateur counterparts. And they use those seconds wisely, determining in that delay how to better approach the play and seeing a higher degree of success because of it.

Eye on the prize

Just as you should take a few moments to consider the end result of any move, it's important to be prepared for life's challenges, and be ready to meet them head-on. That's best accomplished by keeping an eye on the prize.

Most reality-show contestants that become involved in petty arguments with others are the ones to go home, while those who keep focused, aren't distracted and are more likely to win.

[123]

Erase distractions and picture what you want to be as fact.

A personal portrait

By having a clear vision of what you want your life to become, your masterpiece will be a vivid artwork you carry with you wherever you go.

Seeing that picture clearly will help you accomplish the brush strokes required to complete it, whether it's expanding a start-up to rival Google or Facebook or penning a biography on your favorite athlete, who you've studied since he first hit the field playing for your hometown team.

"You can't put a limit on anything," said Phelps in his book, "No Limits." "The more you dream, the farther you get. I think anything is possible if you put your mind, work, and time into it."

Phelps knew from the first time he set foot in the pool that swimming would be his masterpiece.

He saw it clearly, he set the goals he needed to accomplish in order to get there, and then he made the leap, jumping into the deep end and giving it his all, every single time.

[124]

"If I didn't swim my best, I'd think about it at school, at dinner, with my friends. It would drive me crazy," Phelps said.

Only by devoting himself totally to his craft was he able to bring home Olympic medals. He worked hard until swimming had become second nature, putting in the effort required to make sure he was the best he could possibly be.

That focus and drive – with clear goals in mind – were his insurance policy that led him to his place as a national treasure.

Call to action

Create a clear vision of what you want your life to become, what your future will look like, and what it will be like having achieved your goal. Carry your golden vision with you wherever you go.

Once you've painted your vision, set clear goals. Map out a path that will take you from start to finish. Envision yourself moving along that path until you reach your golden vision.

Negative thoughts and doubts have no place in your future or vision. Either use them to your advantage, thereby making them a positive, or erase them completely. Also, be sure to also erase distractions.

Picture what you want and keep your eye on the prize, the golden vision you created for yourself.

How does this apply to your life?

_____

_____

_____

_____

_____

HAPPINESS AND ITS IMPORTANCE

"The path to eternal happiness can be found in the eternal love for someone."

The most important step toward making your dreams a reality is to approach them from a happy place or point of reference.

It might seem impossible – how can I be happy if my dreams are still not my reality? But creating an environment where happiness is present is vital to erasing negative energy. And that gives you the strength required to make your dreams come true.

Nothing can happen in a place of negativity. A gloom-and-doom mentality drives away those who love you, and the sense of loneliness that follows is not conducive to GREATNESS.

Instead, you need to expect happiness, and open your heart to the idea that good things can be yours.

Misery loves company

If happiness is hard to come by, look around you for a minute. If you're surrounded by people who are not happy themselves, it is bound to rub off a bit.

Help them find their bliss and yours will likely follow. On the other hand, some people are just happy being miserable. It sounds crazy, but it's true. For these folks, "unhappy" is the "new happy." They just don't know how to function without drama and problems. What should you do when you're dealing with someone like that? Get out of dodge. Stay clear of them. You might have to let someone else help them, like a professional or a doctor.

Life is here today, but will be gone before you know it. And the time you have here is much too short to spend it feeling miserable or being in the company of miserable people.

Finding happiness

So, if you've already freed yourself from the company of life's "unhappy" people, you can do a few other things to boost the happiness quotient in your life. An excellent way to feel happy is to surround yourself with things that make you smile.

1. Communing with nature can make you feel more at peace and at ease with your surroundings, no matter the challenges.

[128]

2. Helping others, especially those less fortunate, can awaken a sense of purpose and can also offer a better appreciation for those things you do have.

3. Children tend to be intrinsically happy, so surrounding yourself with young people – whether as a Big Brother or Sister or as a parent leader of the Scouts – can help you unleash your own sense of joy.

4. Pets are a great way to boost your feelings of happiness, in part because they offer unconditional love, but also because many require daily exercise, which is also a big boost to good spirits. Volunteer at a local shelter or even adopt your own pet if it fits your lifestyle.

5. Hit the local comedy club for a night of laughter to lift your heart.

Field of passion

One of the best ways to immediately boost your happiness deals with your vocation, career, or business.

Too often people make the conscious decision to work hard at a career or in a business that they don't love. They tell themselves that someday in the future they'll do what they really love. Unfortunately, that "someday" doesn't come along for most of these folks. So in essence, they trade a happy life for a miserable one.

[129]

Interestingly, most successful and wealthy people love what they do. They didn't succeed by working in a dreaded occupation, but rather a passionate career.

Your heart has to be in your work. Passion is a necessary ingredient to success. Passionate entrepreneurs and executives are also very happy people. Why wouldn't they be? They get paid extraordinarily well to do something they enjoy.

Take the late Steve Jobs, founder of Apple, Inc., for example. Jobs loved what he did so much that he continued working even after he became ill. Here's a guy worth billions of dollars. He certainly wasn't working for the money. That's passion. That's happiness.

Call to action

Putting off your happiness may very well be killing your dreams. Make sure you are working in a field of passion. If not, start heading in that direction.

1. Start reading books in your area of interest. Purchase or borrow books from the library. Right now, begin learning about what excites you.

2. Meet people that are like-minded or have already achieved your current dream or goal. Ask them for advice and tips.

3. Everyday take one action that moves your closer to your ideal vocation. You'll be happier for it and you'll begin attracting the resources you need to become great.

How does this apply to your life?

_____

_____

_____

_____

_____

CONCRETE STEPS TOWARD YOUR OUTCOME

"You have to believe that momentum will come your way and when it does you have to capitalize on it."

No matter how firmly in place your mission might seem, nothing can happen when you are trapped in inertia. You just have to get moving.

Just do it

When Nike debuted the slogan "Just do it," they likely had a football player like Kevin Greene in mind.

He began his move toward NFL GREATNESS in high school. Greene played both football and basketball, honing his muscles in a bid to take his athletic career beyond high school to college. He likely always imagined how his life would be, and he did the work required to make it happen.

[132]

At Auburn University, he earned the Defensive Player of the Year award, which attracted the attention of first the Los Angeles Rams and later the Pittsburgh Steelers.

He worked hard, and put in the work, one step at a time.

Living on a prayer

While it is healthy to have faith that God will bring good things your way, you cannot just sit back and wait for prayers to be answered. God gave you the tools to make your dreams come true. You just have to use them.

Have you ever heard the joke about the guy in the flood? Driven to his home's rooftop to escape the rising water, he was passed by a boat. When the man at the helm of the boat told him to get in, the man on the roof said no, God was sending a miracle. The water kept rising and a second boat came by offering assistance. The man again said no, God was sending a miracle. When the water had risen up to his chin, a helicopter flew overhead and the pilot tossed down a rope ladder. For the third time, the man on the roof refused help and said he expected a miracle from God. A few minutes later, when he got to the pearly gates, the man was grouchy with St. Peter and angry God hadn't sent the miracle he expected. St. Peter responded, "I don't know what you're complaining about. We sent two boats and a helicopter."

Don't live your life by prayer alone. Use what you have, whatever it is. Take concrete steps as often as possible to move toward your desired outcome.

Call to action

Small steps make a big difference. Take action even if the results are slow in coming. Small steps will make a big difference in the long run.

Look at it this way. At least you're moving forward, rather than standing completely still.

- Take every opportunity to move in the direction of your GREATNESS or dream.

- Don't expect or attempt to succeed by prayer alone. Pray and get moving. God may have already given you everything you need to succeed; you just have to use what you have.

- Move forward even if you only take small steps initially. Gradually you'll begin to make giant strides and soon you'll find that you've actually achieved your desired outcome.

What are your dreams?

_____

_____

_____

_____

_____

THE SPECIAL ABILITY IN US ALL

"Every day tell yourself 'I can do it,' then when that day comes tell yourself 'I did it.'"

There is a winner inside you just waiting to get out. When you were born, you arrived with all the world's possibilities there for the taking.

God means for you to achieve everything that is possible, but sometimes the world gets in your way.

You are meant for GREATNESS

Realize that no matter the goal, you are capable of GREATNESS.

Charlie Strong had a lot to live up to. With a name like his, he inspired images of brute strength and a host of expectations. He lived up to his name by playing four years for the Florida Gators and then having a coaching career that included decades of helping others to find their inner Hercules. He no doubt told his players to forget imagined limitations and to go for it.

[135]

Power blocks

While you might experience life occurrences that prevent you from reaching your full potential on your desired timeline, you can overcome anything by challenging your inner warrior. Four common "power blocks" that hinder your ability to do this are financial, health, relationships, and self-doubt.

1. **Financial problems** can make you feel helpless and unwilling to leave a dead-end job. However, only with risks can you make changes that will truly transform the circumstances.

2. **Health problems** can make you feel too depleted of energy to make transformations. Take extra steps to improve your health. Hit the gym to drop the extra pounds that make you feel sluggish. Eat better to help improve your cholesterol. Your body is the most valuable piece of equipment money can't buy. Take care of it or your health just might prevent you from sharing your special ability with the world. .

3. **Relationship issues** can make you feel equally helpless. Whether you're alone and lonely or feeling trapped in a relationship that doesn't offer support, it can be draining. So get out there and find a soul mate or tell your unsupportive partner

[136]

to shape up or ship out. You need buoys, not anchors.

4. **Self-doubt** is the most crippling of all, since it can turn dreams into despair in seemingly seconds. Believe in your ability and use positive affirmations to counter any negative thoughts.

These four very common obstacles often distract you from using your special abilities. Once you realize you can overcome and avoid these blockages, you'll be on your way to unleashing your inner warrior and that special ability within.

Call to action

Resolve that nothing will stop you from reaching your full potential, including any of life's problems or issues.

What are your dreams?

_____

_____

_____

_____

_____

Post-Game

"Your thoughts and actions can be your daily wisdom for greatness."

FOCUS ON THE TASK AT HAND

"Every day consists of challenges and times of loneliness that we must overcome in order to drive down the highway of success."

One of the biggest blocks to success is getting distracted and wasting time on insignificant things.

When you sweat the small stuff, you take away focus from the bigger picture and create a roadblock of sorts that makes it harder to achieve your goals.

Stay the course

Every day, take some time to think about what really matters. What's your goal? Anything that isn't directed toward it can wait.

Spending time on non-essentials is like getting mired in quicksand, and just like in the movies, nobody is coming to the rescue. At least not until you sink below the surface, and by then, it's just too late.

[141]

Forget the minutia

Hilary Clinton didn't waste time bemoaning her loss to Barack Obama in her bid for the Democratic presidential nomination in 2008. Complaining then would have been as productive as publicly chastising her husband, then-President Bill Clinton, for his White House dalliances with intern Monica Lewinsky.

So, she played it cool and kept her mouth shut, ultimately landing a key post as the nation's 67th Secretary of State. The first former First Lady to land a post on the presidential cabinet, she now works to assert the nation's core values throughout the world.

For Clinton, staying focused politically and personally has never been in question, and doing so has led to overwhelming personal success.

Work in progress

Hilary Clinton takes steps every day to achieve her own personal goals as well as goals she sees as important for the nation. She tries to see the big picture rather than getting wrapped up in the political minutia that has failed many of her political allies and opponents.

She surrounds herself with people who support her mission, a great way to erase bad vibes and stay focused on the task at hand.

[142]

WIN (What's Important Now)

One of the greatest football coaches of all time, Lou Holtz, developed a powerful principle called WIN. It stands for "what's important now."

Asking yourself that question throughout each day will make sure you stay focused on the "main thing." The key is to tackle the most important things now, putting the rest off until later.

Call to action

Stay the course and overlook all of the minutia. Realize that you and your goals are a work in progress so keep moving and don't quit. Throughout your day, stop and ask yourself what's important now.

Also, ask yourself the WIN question once a week, once a month, and once a quarter. Of course, when looking at larger blocks of time, such as weeks or months, you're attempting to identify what's most important for that period. Without staying focused on your most important goals or tasks, you will easily stray off course, thereby delaying or permanently derailing your dreams.

Always stay focused on the task at hand.

What are your dreams?

_____

_____

_____

_____

_____

GOOD LUCK....BE GREAT

"A man's thoughts can be his daily wisdom for greatness."

As someone extraordinary, you have all the tools you need to get started on your path toward success.

On the day you were born, God gave you the skills, talents, and drive you need to be great. You just need to find a way to put them into play.

You've learned how to give yourself pep talks so you are motivated for another day, and learned that those who try to shut you down are only doing so because they themselves have given up on their dreams. Haters never want to see you rise above them.

Ignore the haters. Get your gear and get going. The game is yours for the winning. You are the Most Valuable Player on your team. Believe in your GREATNESS.

Believe that you are supposed to be, do, and have whatever you desire.

Get started

Your dreams and goals don't stop with belief. They hinge entirely on you and your actions. So take steps toward GREATNESS every day, making moves toward the goal line with every action.

Inertia accomplishes nothing. Idleness, along with self-doubt, has no place in your game plan.

Remember that...

1. Success requires hard work.

2. Those who have what you want know how to get it, so use their experiences as your guide.

3. Setbacks are nothing more than opportunities for learning.

4. Everyone who says you can't is jealous of your success, pure and simple.

5. Enjoy yourself. Have fun all the while. Ultimately, that's what life is all about.

If you enjoyed this book and got at least ONE idea from it I would really love to hear about it. Please email me at kmiinfo@koryminorindustries.com or call our office at (888) 586-1106.

To contact Kory Minor, or to be placed on a mailing list for updates about new programs and information that will help you become great and experience more success, visit his website: www.KoryMinor.com.

Made in the USA
San Bernardino, CA
12 February 2016